FROM TRASH TO TREASURE

PAPER CRAFTS

by Gini Holland

PowerKiDS press™

New York

Published in 2014 by The Rosen Publishing Group, Inc.
29 East 21st Street, New York, NY 10010

First Edition

Produced for Rosen by Ruby Tuesday Books Ltd
Editor for Ruby Tuesday Books Ltd: Mark J. Sachner
US Editor: Kara Murray
Designer: Emma Randall

Photo Credits:
Cover, 1, 3, 4–5, 6–7, 8–9, 10–11, 13 (bottom), 21 (bottom), 23, 25 (bottom), 26, 30–31 © Shutterstock; cover, 1, 12–13, 14–15, 16–17, 18–19, 20–21, 22, 24–25, 27, 28–29, 30–31 © Ruth Owen and John Such.

Library of Congress Cataloging-in-Publication Data

Owen, Ruth, 1967–
 Paper crafts / by Ruth Owen. — First edition.
    pages cm. — (From trash to treasure)
 Includes index.
 ISBN 978-1-4777-1282-5 (library binding) — ISBN 978-1-4777-1358-7 (pbk.) —
 ISBN 978-1-4777-1359-4 (6-pack)
 1. Paper work—Juvenile literature. 2. Salvage (Waste, etc.)—Juvenile literature. I. Title.
 TT870.O955 2014
 731'.2—dc23

                              2012046791

Manufactured in the United States of America

CPSIA Compliance Information: Batch #S13PK8: For Further Information contact Rosen Publishing, New York, New York at 1-800-237-9932

CONTENTS

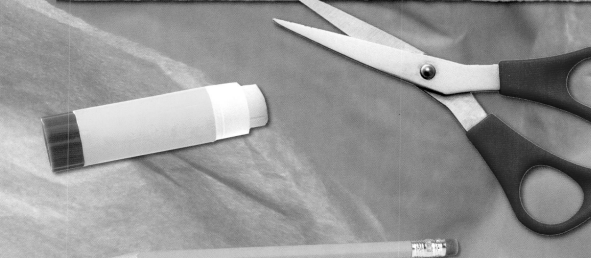

RECYCLE PAPER AND SAVE TREES!

About 90 percent of the paper we use comes from trees.

Live trees do so much for us. They provide oxygen for us to breathe. They also help cool the planet with leafy shade. In fact, many cities are starting to cool their "hot spots" by planting more trees and gardens along their streets, beside railroad tracks, and even on rooftops.

You can help keep more trees alive—so they can cool the planet and give us oxygen—by **recycling** paper. But even recycling takes extra energy. Machines at **paper mills** have to sort different types of paper, remove ink, shred, and turn paper into the **pulp** used to make new paper. It takes energy to run those machines. This book provides six craft projects that let you use your own energy to recycle paper!

When you make crafts from used paper, you can create something new and fun. At the same time, you can help cool the planet. How cool is that?

Saving paper and giving it a second life helps save trees!

These small trees are growing on the roof of a city apartment building.

This paper and cardboard is ready to be shredded and pulped at a paper mill. Then it will be turned into new paper products.

MAGAZINE MASKS

Your magazines may be dog-eared and ready for the recycling bin, but don't toss those fan, fashion, and sports issues—there's life in them yet!

It takes between 8 and 15 trees to make 1 ton (1 t) of magazine paper, depending on the size of the trees. The people who took the photos, designed the pages, and sent the magazine to the printer have all moved on to other projects, but you can give one of those shiny pages another look. Remember that shot of your favorite singer? What about the glossy photo of that gorgeous model, your favorite sports star, or even a beautiful wild animal?

When you make your own mask with a recycled magazine photo, you can disguise yourself as an animal or a famous character for a costume party and help planet Earth.

You will need:

- Old magazines
- Scissors
- One side of a large, empty cereal box
- A glue stick
- A wooden stick or tongue depressor
- Tape
- Yarn pulled from an old scarf or other knitted piece that's ready for reuse or the trash
- Fur from a stuffed animal that's ready for reuse or the trash

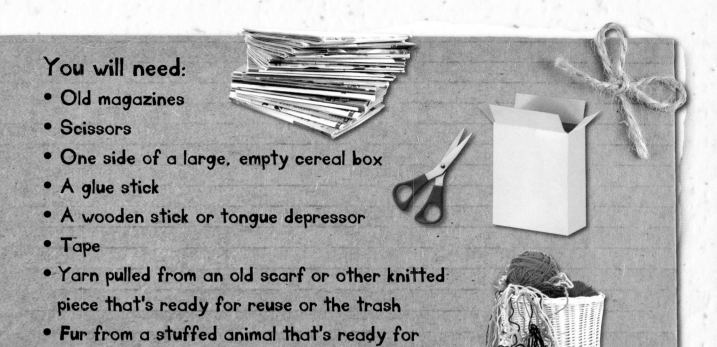

STEP 1:

Look through your old magazines to find a front-facing, life-size face of an animal or famous person. Roughly cut out the face.

STEP 2:
Glue the photo, face up, onto the cardboard from the cereal box.

STEP 3:
Carefully trim off the spare paper and cardboard around the photo.

STEP 4:
Cut around the bottom and sides of the nose on the photo so your own nose can push out. Then cut out two eyeholes or small peepholes to see out of.

STEP 5:
Tape the wooden stick or tongue depressor to the back of the mask so that you can hold the mask up to your face.

STEP 6:
Finally, if you wish, decorate the mask with glued-on yarn or fake fur "hair."

GLOSSY PAPER BEADS

Magazine paper comes directly from freshly cut trees. So when you reuse a magazine, you are the first person to recycle that paper.

In this project, you can create your own beads from recycled glossy magazine pages. Multicolored pages work better than solid-colored or evenly patterned paper. Also, if you want cool black and white beads, try using glossy pages with black type against a white background for a classy look.

When you've made your beads, you can string them together to make your own unique necklaces or bracelets.

You will need:

- A recycled magazine
- A ruler
- A pen or pencil
- Scissors
- A glue stick
- A thin knitting needle, wooden skewer, or toothpick
- String, thick thread, or elastic
- A needle with an eye wide enough for the thread or elastic to pass through

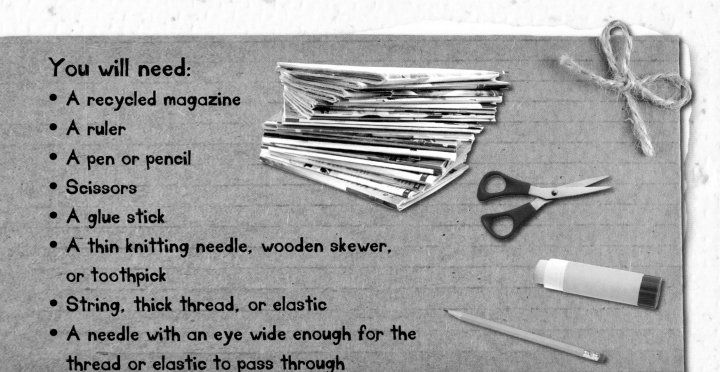

STEP 1:
To make each bead, draw a 9 x 9 x 1 inch (23 x 23 x 2.5 cm) **isosceles triangle** on a magazine page using a ruler and pencil or pen.

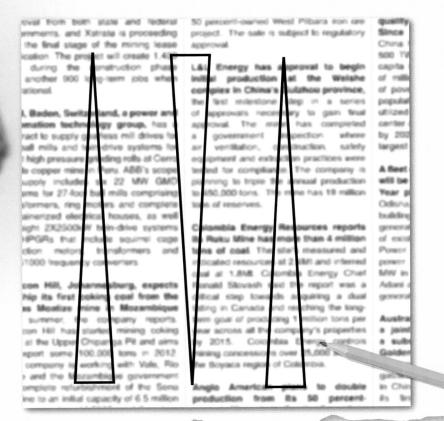

9 inches (23 cm)

1 inch (2.5 cm)

STEP 2:
Cut out the triangle.

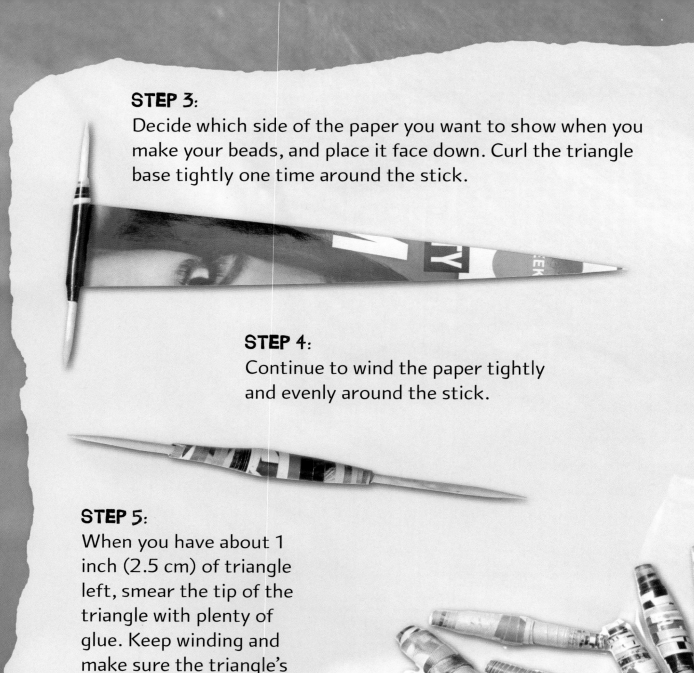

STEP 3:
Decide which side of the paper you want to show when you make your beads, and place it face down. Curl the triangle base tightly one time around the stick.

STEP 4:
Continue to wind the paper tightly and evenly around the stick.

STEP 5:
When you have about 1 inch (2.5 cm) of triangle left, smear the tip of the triangle with plenty of glue. Keep winding and make sure the triangle's tip sticks securely to the rest of the bead.

STEP 6:
Slide the bead off of the stick.

STEP 7:
When you have made as many of these beads as you like, use a needle to thread them onto string, thread, or elastic to make necklaces or bracelets.

GIFT WRAP ORIGAMI PAPER LANTERNS

Do you unwrap your presents carefully and save the paper? Or do you like to just rip the presents open to see what's inside? If you're a "ripper," you might want to change your ways! You may be surprised to see what you can make from that leftover paper.

Each year, Americans dump around 4 million tons (3.5 million t) of gift wrap and shopping bag paper. So cut along taped edges when you open a gift, and save leftover paper when you wrap presents. You can reuse wrapping paper to make your own **origami** paper for mini lanterns.

Make lots! Then slip them over a string of small Christmas lights to brighten up your room.

You will need:

- Recycled gift wrap paper cut into 6 x 6 inch (15 x 15 cm) squares
- A ruler
- Scissors
- A string of small Christmas tree lights

STEP 1:

Place a square of paper white side down. Fold in half toward you, and crease. Unfold, then fold in half the other way, crease, and unfold.

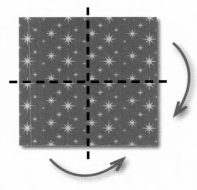

STEP 2:

Now place the paper colored side down. Fold along the dotted line so that point A meets point B, and crease. Unfold, then fold in the other direction so that point C meets point D, and unfold.

STEP 3:

Begin to fold the paper in half toward you along the dotted line. At the same time push points A and B toward each other. The paper will fold to create a triangle.

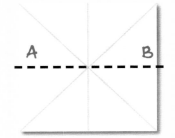

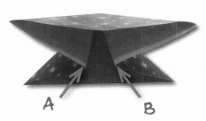

STEP 4:

Fold points A and B up to meet point C along the dotted lines, and crease. Flip the model over and repeat on the other side.

STEP 5:

Fold both side points into the center along the dotted lines, and crease. Flip the model over and repeat.

STEP 6:

You will see that each of the four folds you've just made is actually a little pocket.

Pocket

STEP 7:

Fold down the two top points along the dotted lines. Flip the model over and repeat on the other side.

STEP 8:

Fold in both side points along the dotted lines to create two small triangles. Flip the model over and repeat on the other side.

Triangles

STEP 9:

Now tuck each of the four small triangles you've just made into the pocket beneath it. Press down on each pocket so it is flat and the triangle is snugly inside.

Small triangle

Press down on pocket so it is flat

Pocket

STEP 10:

Now take the model and blow hard into the open end to inflate your lantern.

Final model

Inflated lantern

Blow here

STEP 11:

Finally, carefully slip the open end of the lantern over a bulb on your string of Christmas lights.

PAPIER-MÂCHÉ PIÑATA

Did you know that a lot of the paper used to make newspapers is made from recycled magazines? This paper is called **newsprint**, and when you use it in your art projects, you may be giving another life to a plant that's already served as a tree, a magazine, and a newspaper!

In this project, you can use newspaper to create a **piñata** out of **papier-mâché** for your next party. You will need at least four days to let the piñata dry. Then you can fill it with wrapped hard candies. Get ready for a smashing good time!

You will need:

- Four to six pages from a newspaper
- Extra newspaper to protect your table or counter top
- A balloon
- Two pieces of string approximately 8 feet (2.4 m) long
- A plastic, zip-top baggie
- White glue (mixed three parts glue to one part water)
- A paintbrush
- Colorful paper scraps to decorate the piñata
- Wrapped hard candies

STEP 1:

Tear the newspaper into strips about 1 inch (2.5 cm) wide. Torn edges make a better papier-mâché surface.

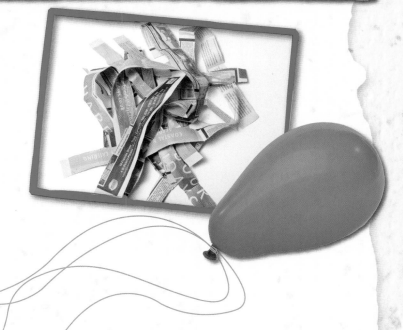

STEP 2:

Blow up the balloon so it's about 14 inches (35 cm) tall.

STEP 3:

Tie each piece of string to the bottom of the balloon. Tie the strings in their centers so you end up with four strands of string hanging from the balloon. Put the strings into the baggie to protect them from the glue.

STEP 4:

Using the paintbrush, brush some of the glue mixture onto the side of the balloon. Lay a strip of newspaper onto the glue, and then brush more glue over the top.

STEP 5:

Repeat this with more newspaper strips, slightly overlapping each strip. Cover the balloon, but leave a small area uncovered at the top. Let the papier-mâché dry for 24 hours.

STEP 6:

Bring the four strings up the side of the balloon and knot them above the hole in the papier-mâché.

STEP 7:

Add a second layer of paper strips, angling them in a different direction than the first layer and covering the strings. Allow to dry for 24 hours.

STEP 8:

Apply a third and then a fourth layer of papier-mâché, allowing each layer to dry for 24 hours.

Now decorate your piñata with scraps of paper—for example used gift wrap paper or tissue paper. Glue or tape the paper scraps to the piñata.

STEP 10:

Pop the balloon through the hole and remove it. Fill the piñata with sweets and then plug the hole with more tissue paper.

STEP 11:

Your piñata is ready to hang up. Have fun!

RECYCLED CANDLEHOLDERS

For this project, you will be recycling some of tissue paper you save from presents and shop bags. Did you know that half the paper in the States is used to wrap and decorate gifts? In from Thanksgiving to New Year's Day, house waste increases 25 percent in the United State

Here is a chance to reuse some of that gift tissu cut back on holiday waste. In addition, you will giving a second life to some glass jars and even up tall candles that have burned down to a sho

You will need:

- Recycled glass jars, such as pickle or spaghetti sauce jars
- Gently used tissue paper
- Scissors
- White glue
- A paintbrush
- Candle stubs or tea lights

STEP 1:

Dig out a smooth glass jar from your recycling bin and wash and dry it thoroughly.

STEP 2:

Cut out shapes, such as squares, from tissue paper. You can make these candleholders as holiday decorations or gifts. Try cutting out tissue hearts for Valentine's Day or snowflakes for Christmas.

STEP 3:

Using the paintbrush, brush some glue onto the outside of the jar. Stick the pieces of tissue paper to the jar.

STEP 4:

Overlap differently colored pieces of tissue paper for a layered effect.

STEP 5:

When the jar is covered with tissue paper, gently brush more glue over the top of the paper. When the glue has dried, your candleholder is ready to use.

STEP 6:

If you are going to put a used candle stub into your jar, light the candle and wait for some wax to melt. Blow out the candle and then gently tip the melted wax into the jar. Press the candle stub into the melted wax so it holds the candle in place. Alternatively, put a tea light candle into your candleholder.

PAPER KITES

"Would you like paper or plastic?" If you care about saving the Earth's **natural resources**, you and your family might bring along your own recycled bags when you go food shopping. Even when you do that, those bags tend to pile up at home in spite of your best efforts. So put them to use!

You can buy beautiful kites in all shapes and sizes, but when you build your own, you can recycle, save money, and tap into your own creativity. Either paper or plastic bags will be great for this project, and all your kite fixings—recycled grocery bags, sticks, tape, string, and ribbon—are easy to find at home. So make a kite and go fly one! Just be sure to stay away from power lines and bad weather.

You will need:

- One 24-inch (60 cm) and one 20-inch (50 cm) straight wooden stick or dowel
- A craft knife
- A ball of string
- Scissors
- A large paper or heavyweight plastic shopping bag
- A ruler
- A pencil
- Duct tape
- Scraps of ribbon

STEP 1:

Lay the sticks on the ground. Use the craft knife to carve a notch, or groove, in both ends of each stick. Be sure the notches are parallel to the ground.

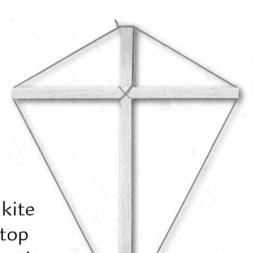

6 inches (15 cm)

10 inches (25 cm)

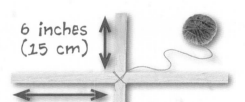

STEP 2:

Place the sticks in a cross, as shown, and bind them tightly together with string in an X pattern.

STEP 3:

Next you will make an outer frame for the kite with the string. Bring the string up to the top notch, thread through, and pull it tight. Continue to thread tightly into the notches around the kite twice. End at the top and tie off.

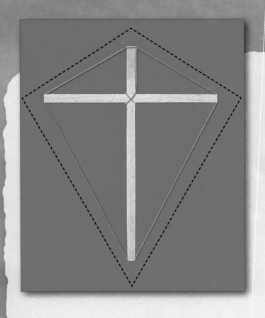

STEP 4:

Cut open the shopping bag to form a large sheet of paper or plastic. You can also cut open and tape two bags together. Place the kite frame onto the paper. Trace a kite shape on the paper that is 2 inches (5 cm) larger than the frame. Cut out.

STEP 5:

Fold the excess paper or plastic back over the frame of the kite and secure with duct tape. You can also add extra tape on each of the four points to strengthen the frame.

Make a small hole on each side of the stick

Bridle

STEP 6:

Make four small holes as shown. Cut a piece of string approximately 35 inches (89 cm) long. Thread the string through the top two holes and knot tightly. Thread the other end through the bottom two holes and knot tightly. This is your kite's bridle.

Make a small hole on each side of the stick

STEP 7:
Cut a 6-foot (2 m) piece of string and stick it to the bottom of the kite with duct tape. Cut the ribbon into sections and tie them into bows spaced evenly on the string. This is the tail that will help your kite fly smoothly.

STEP 8:
The rest of the ball of string is your flying string. Tie the end of it one-third of the way down the bridle. You can retie the flying string higher or lower on the bridle to help your kite fly well. Now, go fly a kite!

You can tie and then wind the ball of string onto a stick if you wish. Then it will unwind easily when you fly the kite.

29

GLOSSARY

isosceles triangle
(eye-sos-LEEZ TRY-ang-gul)
A triangle with two sides of equal length.

natural resources
(NA-chuh-rul REE-sors-ez)
Materials or substances that occur in nature such as wood, rocks, and water.

newsprint (NOOZ-print)
Low-quality, absorbent paper that is made from wood pulp and used for printing newspapers.

origami (or-uh-GAH-mee)
The art of folding paper into decorative shapes or objects.

paper mills (PAY-per MILZ)
Factories where paper is made, either from wood pulp or from waste paper.

papier-mâché
(pay-per-mah-SHAY)
A material made from newspapers and glue that can be molded when it is wet. It hardens as it dries, so it can be used for making models and sculptures.

piñata (peen-YAH-tuh)
A container filled with candy, and sometimes toys, that is hung up so that people can try to break it open using sticks.

pulp (PULP) Fibers from wood that have been turned into a soft, mushy substance, either with the use of chemicals or machines, which is then used to make paper. Alternatively, a soft, mushy substance made from waste paper.

recycling (ree-SY-kling) Turning used materials into new products.

WEBSITES

Due to the changing nature of Internet links, PowerKids Press has developed an online list of websites related to the subject of this book. This site is updated regularly. Please use this link to access the list:

www.powerkidslinks.com/ftt/paper/

READ MORE

Henry, Sally and Trevor Cook. *Eco-Crafts*. Make Your Own Art. New York, NY: Rosen Publishing, 2011.

Lewis, Amanda and Jane Kurisu. *The Jumbo Book of Paper Crafts*. Tonawonda, NY: Kids Can Press, 2002.

McGee, Randel. *Paper Crafts for Christmas*. Paper Craft Fun for Holidays. Berkeley Heights, NJ: Enslow Publishers, Inc., 2009.

INDEX

SOUTH FULTON BRANCH
Atlanta-Fulton Public Library